ICED TEA

REINVENTED

50 creative and delicious recipes for
TAKEYA® Loose Leaf Iced Teas and
TAKEYA® Iced Tea System

John Lown

ICED TEA JUST GOT COOL™

Published by TAKEYA® USA
214 5th Street, #204
Huntington Beach, CA 92648
www.TakeyaUSA.com

ISBN: 978-0-9856441-0-9
First printing 2014

Library of Congress Cataloging-in-Publication data is available

AUTHOR
John Lown

RECIPE DEVELOPER
Alexis Siemons

**ART DIRECTOR,
PHOTO STYLIST**
Binh Phan

BOOK DESIGNER
Grace Tjoa

PHOTOGRAPHER
James Chou

**PHOTO RETOUCHING,
COLOR CORRECTION**
James Chou Photography

FOOD STYLIST
Alise Arato

PROP STYLIST
Kira Vollman-DeBlasis

THANKS!

Thank you Alexis Siemons for your contributions in developing all of the delicious iced tea recipes and thank you TAKEYA team for testing each and every one.

An extra thanks to Photographer James Chou, Photography Producer Kelley Chou and Art Director Binh Phan for capturing the full beauty of the delicious iced tea recipes.

FLASH CHILL ICED TEA DRINK TASTERS

John Lown

Alexis Siemons

Arjun Dua

Binh Phan

Cheri Tennill

Desiree Cooper

Elton Perkins

Grace Tjoa

Mure Browning

Nisha Chawla

Stuart Lown

Sumi Israchanpanich

Tim Hoang

contents

why reinvent iced tea?

Years ago, during a business trip, I took a stroll through a market in Japan and was struck by something you don't see at home in the states. Barrel after barrel overflowing with every loose leaf tea imaginable. Classic black teas. Delicate green teas. Herbal mint teas. The colors, the scent, rich and inviting. To a tea lover like myself, it was nirvana. But it made me think.

You see, iced tea is my passion. I've come to love it way more than any plain glass of water, sweetened soda or sugary juice. Yet there I was, brewing iced tea with ordinary tea bags like most of us do, unaware of the intensely rich experience I was missing.

As I stood in that Japanese market, inhaling the crisp scent, it hit me. Why not make iced teas using these wonderful loose leaf teas?

I began to experiment. My early efforts at loose leaf iced tea brewing tasted considerably better than bagged tea, but they were messy and time consuming.

So my team began designing different methods of making loose leaf iced tea. After several prototypes, we succeeded in creating a fast and easy way to make delicious iced tea beverages

with loose leaf teas. The TAKEYA Flash Chill® Iced Tea Maker, which not only brews loose leaf tea, it flash chills it in just 30 seconds (for details, see page 13).

And we didn't stop there. We created pre-portioned loose leaf tea packets that ensure the perfect pitcher of iced tea every time. Plus we designed accessories including a Citrus Juicer and Fruit Infuser that make it easy to add natural fruit flavors as they strike your fancy.

The Flash Chill® Iced Tea Maker, pre-portioned Loose Leaf Iced Teas and Accessories comprise what we fondly call the TAKEYA Way. It's an iced tea system, designed to enable you to make delicious, nutritious loose leaf iced tea beverages at home, quickly and easily.

We hope you'll come to love these recipes and the ease of making them as much as we do, and share them with your family and friends.

To your health,

John

John Lown

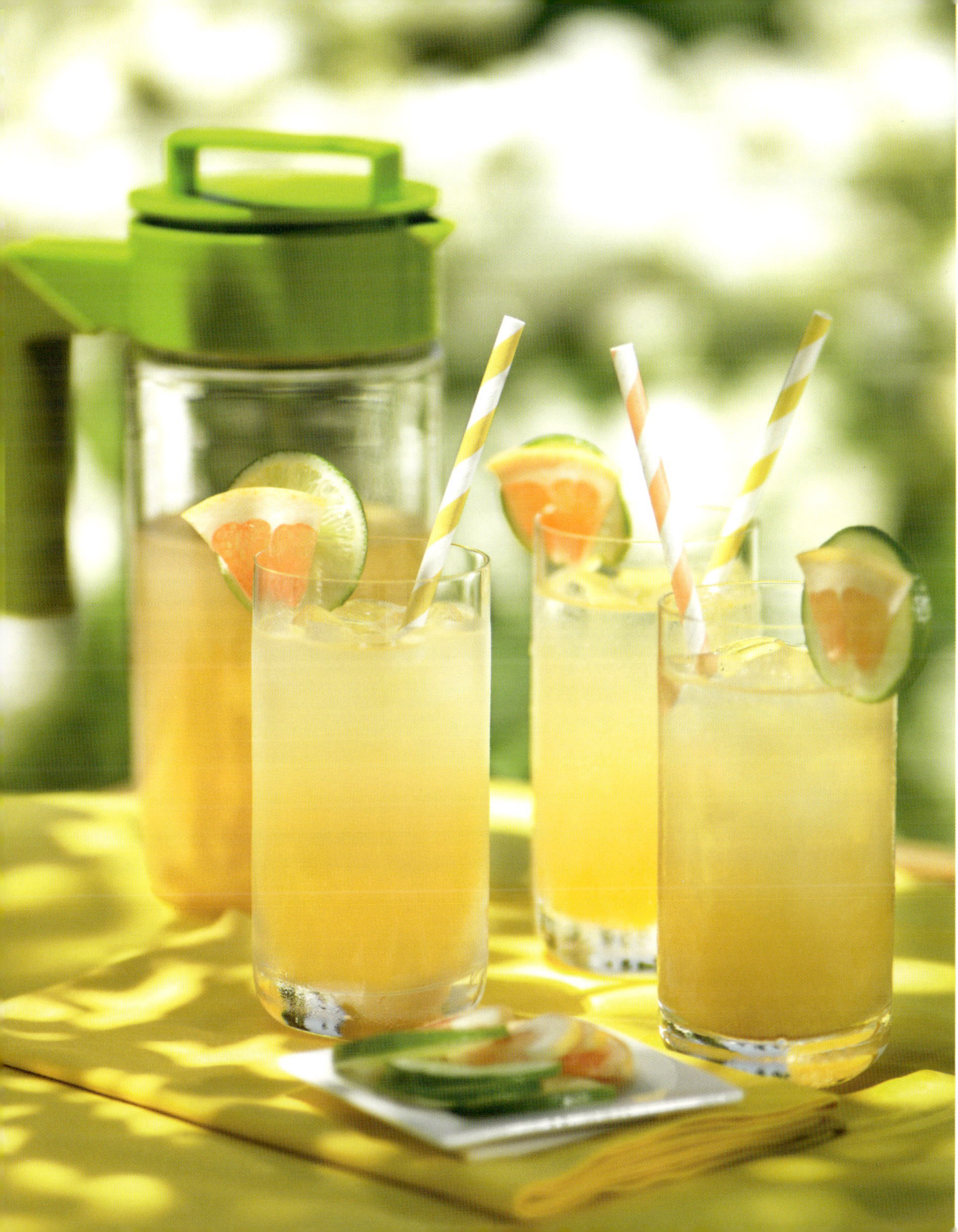

THE
FLASH CHILL®
TECHNOLOGY
EXPLAINED

30-second flash chill technology

Freshly brewed to ice cold in 30 seconds.

hot tea &
ice converge
to release
a refreshing
aromatic flavor

freshly brewed
to ice cold in
30 seconds!

HOW THE FLASH CHILL® TECHNOLOGY WORKS

First, hot water flows over the tea leaves while allowing them to move freely and open fully, releasing their flavor to create a concentrated brew. Next, ice goes in and the airtight lid seals the chamber to retain all the flavor and aroma. Shaking the iced tea maker for 30 seconds melts the ice, chills the tea and dilutes it to the perfect strength. The result is a full pitcher of perfectly brewed iced tea, ready to serve.

THE
FLASH
CHILL
ICED TEA
MAKER,
LOOSE
LEAF TEAS
AND MORE

TAKEYA FLASH CHILL ICED TEA BEVERAGE SYSTEM INCLUDES...

the flash chill iced tea maker

The Flash Chill® Iced Tea Maker does the brewing, and TAKEYA's premium loose leaf teas and accessories let you create an endless variety of delicious natural iced tea beverages — and enjoy them any time, any place.

2 quart/half gallon capacity

loose leaf teas and accessories

loose leaf
iced tea T-PACs™

infuser stand

fruit infuser

citrus juicer

thermo jacket™

16 oz. glass beverage bottles

TAKEYA ICED TEA REINVENTED

2 quart/half gallon iced tea maker

lid

Seals airtight to lock in flavor and aroma, and enables you to store the iced tea maker on its side to save space.

non-slip silicone handle

Soft touch makes it easy to grip and carry.

tea infuser

Fine mesh and roomy, the Tea Infuser provides ample room for loose leaf teas and herbal blends to expand and release their full flavors.

pitcher

Made from FDA-approved, BPA-free acrylic that withstands temperatures from boiling hot to ice cold without cracking or breaking. Stain-proof, odor-proof and cloud-proof.

TAKEYA TIP

To remove tea leaves from the Tea Infuser, turn it upside down and tap on the sink under running water. For deep cleaning, soak in a 50/50 solution of water and hydrogen peroxide or white vinegar and rinse. Note: Compost used tea leaves with your food scraps.

loose leaf
iced tea T-PACs

perfect portions

Our premium quality loose leaf tea is the heart of the recipes in *Iced Tea Reinvented*, and our exclusive pre-portioned T-PACs make it easy to brew the perfect pitcher of iced tea every time.

Each T-PAC contains premium loose leaf tea, foil sealed at the source to ensure tea is at its peak of flavor and aroma when you open it.

enchanted black

tropical black

spring green

mintopia green

coconut vibe

hibiscus pomegranate

accessories for brewing and juicing...

citrus juicer

Juice citrus directly into iced tea for a delicious burst of fresh-squeezed flavor. Simply screw the juicer into the Iced Tea Maker, slice the fruit, press and twist. Designed to collect pits and pulp for easy cleanup. Dishwasher safe.

infuser stand

The Infuser Stand holds the Tea Infuser upright on the countertop during filling or storing. It also prevents drips when you remove the Tea Infuser after brewing.

...and infusing and keeping it cold

thermo jacket

Made of 100% neoprene, the Thermo Jacket zips onto the Iced Tea Maker to keep beverages cold for up to 3 hours. It also absorbs condensation, prevents dripping and protects house-hold surfaces. Available in 1 and 2 quart sizes.

fruit infuser

Use the Fruit Infuser to add fresh fruit flavors to a pitcher of iced tea for a naturally sweet and healthy sip. Fill with sliced or chopped fresh fruits and herbs, twist into the Iced Tea Maker's lid and refrigerate for at least 3 hours. Can also be used to make fruit-infused water. See recipes starting on page 106.

iced tea
on the go

glass bottles

If you love the taste and convenience of bottled drinks but hate the calories and long shelf lives of prepackaged drinks, use TAKEYA glass bottles instead. They're an easy way to take your iced tea beverages to work, school, the gym, and on the road. Make several pitchers of your favorite iced tea recipes, fill the bottles and store in the fridge so they're ready for you and your family to grab and go. Our eco-friendly, refillable glass bottles feature an airtight cap and a silicone jacket that offers a soft grip while protecting the bottle. Dishwasher safe. No need to remove the jacket for cleaning.

HOW TO
BREW
PERFECT
ICED TEA

start with flavorful loose leaf tea

TAKEYA brings you premium loose leaf teas from around the world. Their rich flavors are naturally preserved in T-PACs sealed at the source and conveniently portioned to make a perfect pitcher of iced tea every time.

ENCHANTED BLACK
(loose leaf Assam black tea)

Grown in the famous tea-producing region in Northeast India, Assam black tea brews to a classically brisk, smooth taste with hints of fruit. It's a great base tea for milk and honey and strong fruit-infused flavors.

TROPICAL BLACK
(loose leaf black tea blend and fruit)

Papaya, mango, pineapple and coconut pieces add a tropical burst of fresh flavor to this brisk South Indian tea blend. An aromatic delight, this full-flavored tea blend pairs perfectly with nearly any fresh fruit flavor.

SPRING GREEN
(loose leaf Sencha green tea)

The Chinese Sencha Green Tea brews to a crisp, light and clean flavor. The delicately steamed long tea leaves need to be brewed in water that is hot, but not boiling.

MINTOPIA GREEN
(loose leaf gunpowder
green tea and mint)

Hand-rolled and slightly smoky
gunpowder green tea gets
its name from its resemblance
to small gunpowder pellets.
These little pearls open up
in the infuser, emitting
fresh flavors of green tea
blended with spearmint
and peppermint.

COCONUT VIBE
(premium herb and
fruit blend)

Earthy Green Rooibos blends
with rich coconut, papaya,
pineapple and zesty lime peel
to (nearly) transport you to
the tropics. Harvested in
South Africa, the caffeine-
free leaves brew to a smooth
and grassy flavor.

HIBISCUS POMEGRANATE
(premium herb and
fruit blend)

The rich, tart citrus taste of
hibiscus and pomegranate are
balanced by fruity and sweet
flavors of apple and cherry.
Known for their vibrant red
color, dried hibiscus flowers
brew to a deep red hue that
glows in the pitcher.

water wisdom

We may take water for granted, but when making iced tea it's an important ingredient. For the best flavor, brew loose leaf teas with filtered water to reveal their most subtle flavor characteristics and extract their complex essences.

perfect water temperatures

While water must be hot to help tea leaves release their flavors, not all teas need boiling water to extract the flavor.

Loose leaf green tea is best brewed in water that has cooled after boiling – a full boil can burn the leaves and give tea a bitter taste. Black teas and herbal blends need almost boiling water to reveal their true flavors.

Water temperatures are included in every recipe, but you can also use the guide below. You don't need a thermometer — just a clock.

These are brewing temperatures for TAKEYA loose leaf tea and herbal blends. Other teas may vary.

Black Tea: Heat water to a boil and let cool for one minute before brewing.

Green Tea: Heat water to a boil and let cool for three to four minutes before brewing.

Herbal Tea: Heat water to a boil and let cool for one minute before brewing.

TAKEYA TIP

Avoid heating your water in the microwave. You can't get an exact water temperature this way and won't be able to adjust it for every tea type. It also makes iced tea taste flat.

best brewing times

Timing truly is everything when it comes to perfect iced tea. For just the right amount of flavor intensity, each type of tea requires a specific brew time, ranging from 3 to 7 minutes.

Whether green, black, oolong or white, each loose leaf tea variety is harvested from the Camellia Sinensis plant. The way in which the delicate leaves are processed determines how they need to be brewed.

As a simple rule of thumb, the more processed the leaves, the hotter the water needs to be to extract the complex flavors lingering within.

Loose leaf tea retains fresh flavors that are released as the leaves unfurl and expand while brewing, and TAKEYA's premium loose tea leaves are so fresh and fragrant that they can be brewed a second time.

brewing instructions

:: **Use 1 Iced Tea Packet per quart** ::

ENCHANTED BLACK	**TROPICAL BLACK**	**SPRING GREEN**	**MINTOPIA GREEN**	**COCONUT VIBE**	**HIBISCUS POMEGRANATE**
Contains caffeine	Contains caffeine	Contains caffeine	Contains caffeine	Caffeine-free	Caffeine-free
Bring water to boil and let cool for 1 minute. Brew for 5 minutes.	Bring water to boil and let cool for 1 minute. Brew for 5 minutes.	Bring water to boil and let cool for 4 minutes. Brew for 3 minutes.	Bring water to boil and let cool for 3 minutes. Brew for 3 minutes.	Bring water to boil and let cool for 1 minute. Brew for 7 minutes.	Bring water to boil and let cool for 1 minute. Brew for 7 minutes.

the path to perfection

Using the TAKEYA Flash Chill® Iced Tea Maker, you can make freshly brewed, loose leaf iced tea in minutes. It'll be ready to drink, rich in flavor and aroma and chilled to the perfect temperature. Just follow these simple steps, to make a 2 quart pitcher of your favorite iced tea.

CHOOSE TEA PACKET

- Open and pour the contents of 2 TAKEYA iced tea packets into the Tea Infuser (for a 2 quart pitcher).

ADD HOT WATER

- Boil 1 quart (4 cups) of water in kettle or saucepan and let cool for the recommended time.

- Fill pitcher halfway with hot water.

BREW

- Screw the Tea Infuser into the lid, using the Infuser Extender, and lower it into the water. Twist the lid partially closed, allowing steam to vent. Brew for the recommended time. This will make a concentrated brew.

TAKEYA TIP

Save brewed tea leaves in the Tea Infuser and place in the Infuser Stand. Brew a second time to make another pitcher of iced tea. Just be sure to use the brewed tea leaves within 30 minutes and add an extra minute to the original brew time.

serve and enjoy!

REMOVE THE TEA INFUSER

- Twist and lift the lid and Tea Infuser out of the pitcher. To avoid drips, rest the Tea Infuser in the Infuser Stand.

- If desired, stir in sweetener until dissolved.

FLASH CHILL®

- Fill the pitcher to the top with ice and seal lid airtight. Shake for about 30 seconds or until ice has melted. Your concentrated brew is now the perfect pitcher of ice cold tea.

- Twist the lid open, aligning the arrows with the pour spout. Pour over ice and enjoy!

TAKEYA ICED TEA REINVENTED

ingredients to try

The recipes that follow use a variety of ingredients combined with TAKEYA loose leaf teas. But don't be afraid to experiment. The lists below will give you some ideas and help you get started on a new adventure with freshly brewed, loose leaf iced tea.

sweeteners

While we suggest using rich, natural honey in our recipes, how you sweeten your iced tea is up to you. Don't have honey on hand? Try maple syrup, agave nectar or raw cane sugar. Test a few to find your favorite.

AGAVE EXTRACT

HONEY (WILDFLOWER RECOMMENDED)

RAW CANE SUGAR

MAPLE SYRUP

STEVIA

herbs, spices and nuts

Make your way to a local spice shop or the spice aisle in your grocery store to find these spicy and nutty additions. For the green herbs, pick some from your garden or find them fresh in the produce section of your grocery store.

ALMONDS

BASIL

CARDAMOM PODS

CINNAMON STICKS

CLOVES (WHOLE)

GINGER ROOT

HAZELNUTS

LEMONGRASS

MINT

UNSWEETENED COCONUT FLAKES

VANILLA BEANS

liquids

Beyond the water needed to brew the tea, some recipes call for a special liquid to change the flavor or add a sparkling fizz.

COCONUT WATER

SPARKLING WATER

MILK (SUBSTITUTE: ALMOND MILK)

fruits

For the freshest flavor, try to shop seasonally at your local farmers' market or grocery store. Can't find fresh fruit? Head over to the frozen food

aisle to pick up a bag and defrost before infusing. If you are in a time pinch you can substitute unsweetened fruit juices from your fridge for real fruit, but beware of high sugar and artificial ingredients. In other words, use fresh whenever possible.

BERRIES

BLACKBERRY
BLUEBERRY
CRANBERRY
RASPBERRY
STRAWBERRY
KIWI

MELONS

CANTALOUPE
HONEYDEW
WATERMELON

CITRUS

BLOOD ORANGES
CLEMENTINE
GRAPEFRUIT
LEMON
LIME
ORANGE
TANGERINE

POME FRUIT

APPLES (GREEN & RED)
PEAR

STONE FRUIT

APRICOT
CHERRY
PEACH
PLUM

TROPICAL FRUIT

COCONUT
LYCHEE
MANGO
PAPAYA
PINEAPPLE
POMEGRANATE

perfect food pairings

Premium loose leaf teas and fruit infusions are like fine wines. They can be a perfect accompaniment to foods, from barbeque to grilled seafood and fine cheeses to rich desserts.

These are some general pairing principles:

Stronger black teas with berry infusions stand up well to hearty red meat dishes and barbeque.

Green teas with delicate melon or citrus notes pair well with salads, grilled seafood and ceviche.

Tropical rooibos with pineapple and coconut infusions complement cold soups and Caribbean-inspired cuisine.

The creamy, spiced flavors of our Spiced Chai Latte recipe are a good match with spiced cakes and cookies.

You'll find more ideas for food pairings in specific recipes. But really, it's hard to go wrong with loose leaf iced teas, with breakfast, lunch, dinner or any time.

TAKEYA ICED TEA REINVENTED

enchanted black

This hearty black tea brews to a classically brisk, smooth flavor that works as a perfect base for milk and honey and bold fruit flavors. Our Enchanted Black tea recipes are filled with fresh fruits, flavorful spices and herbs. Enjoy alone or paired with your favorite meal.

Iced tea just got cool™

INGREDIENTS

FOR 2 QUART
ICED TEA MAKER

Makes 8 glasses

8 cinnamon sticks

6-inch piece ginger, thinly sliced

2 teaspoons whole cloves

2 TAKEYA Enchanted Black Iced Tea Packets

4½ cups milk (substitute: almond milk)

1 teaspoon ground cardamom

6 tablespoons honey

Ice

spiced chai latte

This fresh take on the Indian Masala Chai tea beverage will make you wonder why you ever liked the syrupy-sweet bottled version. For a spicier sip, add a thinly sliced 6-inch piece of ginger and 8 cinnamon sticks (from Tea Infuser) to the Fruit Infuser, and infuse in the refrigerator for 1 hour.

1. PREP Add cinnamon sticks, sliced ginger and cloves to the Tea Infuser. Tear open the TAKEYA Enchanted Black Iced Tea Packets, pour tea into Tea Infuser and twist into lid.

2. BREW & FLAVOR Heat milk to a boil and fill the pitcher halfway. Lower the lid with attached Tea Infuser into the hot milk, allowing steam to vent, and brew for 15 minutes. Remove the lid and detach the Tea Infuser. Stir in ground cardamom and honey until dissolved.

3. FLASH CHILL Top off with ice, seal lid and shake for 30 seconds to flash chill. Zip on the Thermo Jacket.

FOOD PAIRING *Serve rich, buttery breakfast treats like French toast, frittata and banana bread with this sweet and nutty latte.*

vanilla, hazelnut & cardamom latte

Inspired to swap whole vanilla beans for vanilla extract? Simply slice open and scrape out seeds from 4 beans. Mix the tiny seeds into the hot milk and pop the empty pods into the Fruit Infuser with the nuts for added flavor.

1. PREP Add chopped hazelnuts and almonds to a pan and toast over medium-low heat for 3 minutes (until nuts begin to brown). Tear open the TAKEYA Enchanted Black Iced Tea Packets and pour tea into Tea Infuser. Add 8 tablespoons of the mixed toasted nuts to the Tea Infuser and twist into lid.

2. BREW Heat milk to a boil and fill the pitcher halfway. Lower the lid with attached Tea Infuser into the hot milk, allowing steam to vent, and brew for 15 minutes. Remove the lid and detach the Tea Infuser. Stir in vanilla extract, ground cardamom and honey.

3. FLASH CHILL Top off with ice, seal lid and shake for 30 seconds to flash chill. Remove 1⅓ cup of the iced latte to make room for the infusion.

4. ADD NUT FLAVOR Twist the Fruit Infuser into the Infuser Extender and add the 10 remaining tablespoons of toasted nuts to the Fruit Infuser. Twist the Fruit Infuser into the lid, lower it into the iced tea latte and seal airtight. Zip on the Thermo Jacket and infuse for 3 hours in the refrigerator before serving.

INGREDIENTS

FOR 2 QUART
ICED TEA MAKER
Makes 8 glasses

10 tablespoons hazelnuts, chopped

8 tablespoons almonds, chopped

2 TAKEYA Enchanted Black Iced Tea Packets

4½ cups milk (substitute: almond milk)

5 teaspoons pure vanilla extract

1 teaspoon ground cardamom

6 tablespoons honey

Ice

INGREDIENTS

FOR 2 QUART
ICED TEA MAKER
Makes 8 glasses

**2 TAKEYA Enchanted
Black Iced Tea Packets**

**4 cups cold water,
preferably filtered**

Ice

2 oranges

5 cinnamon sticks

**2½ cups red apple,
chopped into
½-inch pieces**

(Optional: extra cinnamon
sticks for garnish)

apple, orange & cinnamon

Cinnamon sticks add just the right touch of spice to this sweet and brisk infusion. For an extra kick of flavor, garnish each glass with a cinnamon stick.

1. PREP Tear open the TAKEYA Enchanted Black Iced Tea Packets, pour tea into Tea Infuser and twist into lid.

2. BREW Heat water to a boil, cool for 1 minute and fill the pitcher halfway. Lower the lid with attached Tea Infuser into the hot water, allowing steam to vent, and brew for 5 minutes. Remove the lid and detach the Tea Infuser.

3. FLASH CHILL Top off with ice, seal lid and shake for 30 seconds to flash chill. Remove 2⅓ cups of the iced tea to make room for the fruit infusion.

4. ADD CITRUS FLAVOR Twist the Citrus Juicer into the top of the pitcher and juice the oranges. Twist off the Citrus Juicer, seal and shake to mix.

5. ADD FRUIT & SPICE FLAVORS Twist the Fruit Infuser into the Infuser Extender and add cinnamon sticks and chopped apples. Twist the Fruit Infuser into the lid, lower it into the iced tea and seal airtight. Zip on the Thermo Jacket and infuse for 3 hours in the refrigerator before serving.

FAST JUICE ALTERNATIVE *Add 6 cinnamon sticks to the Tea Infuser along with the contents of the TAKEYA Enchanted Black Iced Tea Packets, and follow the steps above to brew and chill the tea. Remove 2 cups of the iced tea. Add 1¼ cup chilled apple juice and ¾ cup chilled orange juice. Seal lid and shake to mix before serving.*

INGREDIENTS

FOR 2 QUART
ICED TEA MAKER
Makes 8 glasses

**2 TAKEYA Enchanted
Black Iced Tea Packets**

**4 cups cold water,
preferably filtered**

3 tablespoons honey

Ice

**4-inch piece ginger,
thinly sliced**

**2¼ cups peaches,
chopped into
½-inch pieces**

peach & ginger

The classically sweet and spicy flavors of peach and ginger balance each other in this refreshing iced tea sip.

1. PREP Tear open the TAKEYA Enchanted Black Iced Tea Packets, pour tea into Tea Infuser and twist into lid.

2. BREW Heat water to a boil, cool for 1 minute and fill the pitcher halfway. Lower the lid with attached Tea Infuser into the hot water, allowing steam to vent, and brew for 5 minutes. Remove the lid and detach the Tea Infuser. Stir in honey until dissolved.

3. FLASH CHILL Top off with ice, seal lid and shake for 30 seconds to flash chill. Remove 1⅓ cups of the iced tea to make room for the fruit infusion.

4. ADD FRUIT FLAVOR Twist the Fruit Infuser into the Infuser Extender and add sliced ginger and chopped peaches. Twist the Fruit Infuser into the lid, lower it into the iced tea and seal airtight. Zip on the Thermo Jacket and infuse for 3 hours in the refrigerator before serving.

FAST JUICE ALTERNATIVE *Add sliced ginger to the bottom of the pitcher and muddle with a wooden spoon. Follow the steps above to brew, sweeten and chill the iced tea. Remove 2 cups of the iced tea. Add 2 cups unsweetened and chilled peach juice. Seal lid and shake to mix before serving.*

blood orange lemonade

Try this twist on the classic half tea & half lemonade. Blood oranges add a sweet tang and vibrant color.

1. PREP Tear open the TAKEYA Enchanted Black Iced Tea Packets, pour tea into Tea Infuser and twist into lid.

2. BREW Heat water to a boil, cool for 1 minute and fill the pitcher halfway. Lower the lid with attached Tea Infuser into the hot water, allowing steam to vent, and brew for 5 minutes. Remove the lid and detach the Tea Infuser. Stir in honey until dissolved.

3. FLASH CHILL Top off with ice, seal lid and shake for 30 seconds to flash chill. Remove 1 cup of the iced tea to make room for the citrus juice.

4. ADD CITRUS FLAVOR Twist the Citrus Juicer into the top of the pitcher and juice the lemon and blood oranges. Twist off the Citrus Juicer, seal and shake to mix before serving. Zip on the Thermo Jacket.

INGREDIENTS

FOR 2 QUART
ICED TEA MAKER
Makes 8 glasses

2 TAKEYA Enchanted Black Iced Tea Packets

4 cups cold water, preferably filtered

8 tablespoons honey

Ice

1 lemon

4 blood oranges

ENCHANTED BLACK

apricot & plum

If this stone fruit infusion is your go-to sip, be sure to add extra apricot and plums to your basket as they can be difficult to find beyond summer months. Slice and freeze the seasonal fruit for year-round enjoyment.

1. PREP Tear open the TAKEYA Enchanted Black Iced Tea Packets, pour tea into Tea Infuser and twist into lid.

2. BREW Heat water to a boil, cool for 1 minute and fill the pitcher halfway. Lower the lid with attached Tea Infuser into the hot water, allowing steam to vent, and brew for 5 minutes. Remove the lid and detach the Tea Infuser. Stir in honey until dissolved.

3. FLASH CHILL Top off with ice, seal lid and shake for 30 seconds to flash chill. Remove 1½ cups of the iced tea to make room for the fruit infusion.

4. ADD FRUIT FLAVOR Twist the Fruit Infuser into the Infuser Extender and add chopped apricot and plum. Twist the Fruit Infuser into the lid, lower it into the iced tea and seal airtight. Zip on the Thermo Jacket and infuse for 3 hours in the refrigerator before serving.

INGREDIENTS

FOR 2 QUART
ICED TEA MAKER

Makes 8 glasses

2 TAKEYA Enchanted Black Iced Tea Packets

4 cups cold water, preferably filtered

3 tablespoons honey

Ice

1⅓ cup apricot, chopped into ½-inch pieces

1½ cup plum, chopped into ½-inch pieces

ENCHANTED BLACK

watermelon & basil

This fruit and herb duo might sound like an unexpected pair, but the sweet watermelon and earthy basil flavors blend exceptionally well with the brisk black tea.

1. PREP Add chopped basil to the bottom of the pitcher and muddle with a wooden spoon. Tear open the TAKEYA Enchanted Black Iced Tea Packets, pour tea into Tea Infuser and twist into lid.

2. BREW Heat water to a boil, cool for 1 minute and fill the pitcher halfway. Lower the lid with attached Tea Infuser into the hot water, allowing steam to vent, and brew for 5 minutes. Remove the lid and detach the Tea Infuser. Stir in honey until dissolved.

3. FLASH CHILL Top off with ice, seal lid and shake for 30 seconds to flash chill. Remove 1½ cups of the iced tea to make room for the fruit infusion.

4. ADD FRUIT FLAVOR Twist the Fruit Infuser into the Infuser Extender and add chopped watermelon. Twist the Fruit Infuser into the lid, lower it into the iced tea and seal airtight. Zip on the Thermo Jacket and infuse for 3 hours in the refrigerator before serving.

FAST BLEND ALTERNATIVE *Add chopped basil to the bottom of the pitcher and muddle with a wooden spoon. Follow the steps above to brew, sweeten and chill the iced tea. Remove 2 cups of the iced tea. Add 2 cups blended watermelon. Seal lid and shake to mix before serving.*

TAKEYA TIP *Use toothpicks to create small fruit and herb kabobs. Simply layer basil leaves and watermelon pieces. Add the garnish to each glass before serving. Just be sure to purchase extra fruit and herbs for this added treat.*

INGREDIENTS

FOR 2 QUART
ICED TEA MAKER

Makes 8 glasses

½ cup fresh basil, chopped

2 TAKEYA Enchanted Black Iced Tea Packets

4 cups cold water, preferably filtered

2 tablespoons honey

Ice

2¾ cups watermelon, chopped into ½-inch pieces

THE NEXT GREAT RECIPE MIGHT BE YOURS

Share your best at

   / TakeyaUSA

ENCHANTED BLACK

tropical black

An aromatic delight, this full-flavored black tea blend pairs perfectly with most any fresh fruit flavor. Before you brew, take note of the beautiful blue safflower petals and pieces of fruit that add bright hints of color to this rich blend. Perfect for hot summer days or star-filled nights on the patio.

Iced tea just got cool™

INGREDIENTS

FOR 2 QUART
ICED TEA MAKER

Makes 8 glasses

**2 TAKEYA Tropical
Black Iced Tea Packets**

**4 cups cold water,
preferably filtered**

4 tablespoons honey

Ice

1 lime

**1½ cups papaya, chopped
into ½-inch pieces**

**1 cup kiwi, chopped into
½-inch pieces**

papaya, kiwi & lime

This tropical trio of flavors easily sends your
senses to the tropics. Perfect for poolside
parties or just when you need to get away...
via your taste buds.

1. PREP Tear open the TAKEYA Tropical Black Iced Tea Packets,
pour tea into Tea Infuser and twist into lid.

2. BREW Heat water to a boil, cool for 1 minute and fill the pitcher
halfway. Lower the lid with attached Tea Infuser into the hot water,
allowing steam to vent, and brew for 5 minutes. Remove the lid and
detach the Tea Infuser. Stir in honey until dissolved.

3. FLASH CHILL Top off with ice, seal lid and shake for 30 seconds
to flash chill. Remove 1¾ cups of the iced tea to make room for the
fruit infusion.

4. ADD CITRUS FLAVOR Twist the Citrus Juicer into the top of the
pitcher and juice the lime. Twist off the Citrus Juicer, seal and shake
to mix.

5. ADD FRUIT FLAVOR Twist the Fruit Infuser into the Infuser
Extender and add chopped papaya and kiwi. Twist the Fruit Infuser into
the lid, lower it into the iced tea and seal airtight. Zip on the Thermo
Jacket and infuse for 3 hours in the refrigerator before serving.

TROPICAL BLACK

papaya, cantaloupe & lime

Using a melon baller, scoop and freeze small cantaloupe balls until solid. Before serving, fill each glass with a few frozen cantaloupe balls (instead of ice) to add extra chill to the tropical infusion.

1. PREP Tear open the TAKEYA Tropical Black Iced Tea Packets, pour tea into Tea Infuser and twist into lid.

2. BREW Heat water to a boil, cool for 1 minute and fill the pitcher halfway. Lower the lid with attached Tea Infuser into the hot water, allowing steam to vent, and brew for 5 minutes. Remove the lid and detach the Tea Infuser.

3. FLASH CHILL Top off with ice, seal lid and shake for 30 seconds to flash chill. Remove 1¾ cups of the iced tea to make room for the fruit infusion.

4. ADD CITRUS FLAVOR Twist the Citrus Juicer into the top of the pitcher and juice the lime. Twist off the Citrus Juicer, seal and shake to mix.

5. ADD FRUIT FLAVOR Twist the Fruit Infuser into the Infuser Extender and add chopped cantaloupe and papaya. Twist the Fruit Infuser into the lid, lower it into the iced tea and seal airtight. Zip on the Thermo Jacket and infuse for 3 hours in the refrigerator before serving.

INGREDIENTS

FOR 2 QUART
ICED TEA MAKER
Makes 8 glasses

2 TAKEYA Tropical Black Iced Tea Packets

4 cups cold water, preferably filtered

Ice

1 lime

1½ cups cantaloupe, chopped into ½-inch pieces

1 cup papaya, chopped into ½-inch pieces

(Optional: extra cantaloupe for garnish)

TROPICAL BLACK

pineapple, mango & mint

Never cut a pineapple? It's easy. Simply place the pineapple on its side and cut off the leaves, crown and stem off of the fruit. Place the pineapple upright and slice off the brown skin until you only have sweet, yellow fruit.

1. PREP Tear open the TAKEYA Tropical Black Iced Tea Packets, pour tea into Tea Infuser and twist into lid.

2. BREW Heat water to a boil, cool for 1 minute and fill the pitcher halfway. Lower the lid with attached Tea Infuser into the hot water, allowing steam to vent, and brew for 5 minutes. Remove the lid and detach the Tea Infuser.

3. FLASH CHILL Top off with ice, seal lid and shake for 30 seconds to flash chill. Remove 1½ cups of the iced tea to make room for the fruit infusion.

4. ADD FRUIT & HERB FLAVOR Twist the Fruit Infuser into the Infuser Extender and add chopped pineapple, mango and fresh mint leaves. Twist the Fruit Infuser into the lid, lower it into the iced tea and seal airtight. Zip on the Thermo Jacket and infuse for 3 hours in the refrigerator before serving.

FAST JUICE ALTERNATIVE *Add 1 cup chopped mint to the bottom of the pitcher and muddle with a wooden spoon. Follow the steps above to brew and chill the iced tea. Remove 2 cups of the iced tea. Add ¾ cup unsweetened and chilled mango juice and 1¼ cup unsweetened and chilled pineapple juice. Seal lid and shake to mix before serving.*

FOOD PAIRING *Pair this tropical and brisk tea with a rich yet sweet pineapple guacamole for an afternoon snack.*

INGREDIENTS

FOR 2 QUART
ICED TEA MAKER

Makes 8 glasses

2 TAKEYA Tropical Black Iced Tea Packets

4 cups cold water, preferably filtered

Ice

1½ cups pineapple, chopped into ½-inch pieces

1 cup mango, chopped into ½-inch pieces

⅔ cup fresh mint, chopped

TROPICAL BLACK

clementine & blood orange

This citrus sip offers a subtly sweet twist on standard oranges. The blood oranges add a pop of vibrant color with crimson hued juice, making it perfect for parties.

INGREDIENTS

FOR 2 QUART
ICED TEA MAKER

Makes 8 glasses

2 TAKEYA Tropical Black Iced Tea Packets

4 cups cold water, preferably filtered

3 tablespoons honey

Ice

12 clementines

4 blood oranges

1. PREP Tear open the TAKEYA Tropical Black Iced Tea Packets, pour tea into Tea Infuser and twist into lid.

2. BREW Heat water to a boil, cool for 1 minute and fill the pitcher halfway. Lower the lid with attached Tea Infuser into the hot water, allowing steam to vent, and brew for 5 minutes. Remove the lid and detach the Tea Infuser. Stir in honey until dissolved.

3. FLASH CHILL Top off with ice, seal lid and shake for 30 seconds to flash chill. Remove 2 cups of the iced tea to make room for the citrus juice.

4. ADD CITRUS FLAVOR Twist the Citrus Juicer into the top of the pitcher and juice the clementines and blood oranges (rinse off Citrus Juicer halfway through juicing to remove pulp and seeds). Twist off the Citrus Juicer, seal and shake to mix before serving. Zip on the Thermo Jacket.

INGREDIENTS

FOR 2 QUART
ICED TEA MAKER

Makes 8 glasses

**2 TAKEYA Tropical
Black Iced Tea Packets**

**4 cups cold water,
preferably filtered**

Ice

**1½ cups peaches, chopped
into ½-inch pieces**

**1¼ cups mango, chopped
into ½-inch pieces**

peach & mango

When searching for a mango to add to your shopping cart, pick the one that gives slightly when squeezed. The stem should have a fresh, fruity aroma.

1. PREP Tear open the TAKEYA Tropical Black Iced Tea Packets, pour tea into Tea Infuser and twist into lid.

2. BREW Heat water to a boil, cool for 1 minute and fill the pitcher halfway. Lower the lid with attached Tea Infuser into the hot water, allowing steam to vent, and brew for 5 minutes. Remove the lid and detach the Tea Infuser.

3. FLASH CHILL Top off with ice, seal lid and shake for 30 seconds to flash chill. Remove 1½ cups of the iced tea to make room for the fruit infusion.

4. ADD FRUIT FLAVOR Twist the Fruit Infuser into the Infuser Extender and add chopped peaches and mango. Twist the Fruit Infuser into the lid, lower it into the iced tea and seal airtight. Zip on the Thermo Jacket and infuse for 3 hours in the refrigerator before serving.

FAST JUICE ALTERNATIVE *Follow the steps above to brew and chill the iced tea. Remove 2½ cups of the iced tea. Add 1 cup unsweetened and chilled mango juice and 1½ cups unsweetened and chilled peach juice. Seal lid and shake to mix before serving.*

kiwi & coconut

Pair this treat with a tropical salad for the perfect lunch or snack. Simply combine sliced kiwi, avocado and mango in a bowl and top with a lime vinaigrette dressing.

1. PREP Tear open the TAKEYA Tropical Black Iced Tea Packets, pour tea into Tea Infuser and twist into lid.

2. BREW Heat water to a boil, cool for 1 minute and fill the pitcher halfway. Lower the lid with attached Tea Infuser into the hot water, allowing steam to vent, and brew for 5 minutes. Remove the lid and detach the Tea Infuser. Stir in honey until dissolved.

3. FLASH CHILL Top off with ice, seal lid and shake for 30 seconds to flash chill. Remove 1⅓ cups of the iced tea to make room for the fruit infusion.

4. ADD FRUIT FLAVOR Twist the Fruit Infuser into the Infuser Extender and add chopped coconut and kiwi. Twist the Fruit Infuser into the lid, lower it into the iced tea and seal airtight. Zip on the Thermo Jacket and infuse for 3 hours in the refrigerator before serving.

FAST FRUIT BLEND ALTERNATIVE *Follow the steps above to brew, sweeten and chill the iced tea. Remove 2¾ cups of the iced tea. Add 2 cups unsweetened and chilled coconut water and ¾ cup blended kiwi. Seal lid and shake to mix before serving.*

INGREDIENTS

FOR 2 QUART
ICED TEA MAKER

Makes 8 glasses

**2 TAKEYA Tropical
Black Iced Tea Packets**

**4 cups cold water,
preferably filtered**

4½ tablespoons honey

Ice

**1¾ cups fresh coconut,
shell removed & chopped
into ½-inch pieces**

**1 cup kiwi, peeled
and chopped into
½-inch pieces**

TROPICAL BLACK

orange & lime

Add extra oranges and limes to your shopping bag, and dehydrate ¼-inch citrus slices on a rack in the oven at 170 degrees for a stained glass effect. Simply heat the slices for 4 hours, turn off the oven and let them cool in the oven overnight. Cut thin slits in the oranges and limes and place them on the rim of each glass before serving.

1. PREP Tear open the TAKEYA Tropical Black Iced Tea Packets, pour tea into Tea Infuser and twist into lid.

2. BREW Heat water to a boil, cool for 1 minute and fill the pitcher halfway. Lower the lid with attached Tea Infuser into the hot water, allowing steam to vent, and brew for 5 minutes. Remove the lid and detach the Tea Infuser. Stir in honey until dissolved.

3. FLASH CHILL Top off with ice, seal lid and shake for 30 seconds to flash chill. Remove 2 cups of the iced tea to make room for the citrus juice.

4. ADD CITRUS FLAVOR Twist the Citrus Juicer into the top of the pitcher and juice the oranges and limes. Twist off the Citrus Juicer, seal and shake to mix before serving. Zip on the Thermo Jacket.

INGREDIENTS

FOR 2 QUART
ICED TEA MAKER

Makes 8 glasses

2 TAKEYA Tropical Black Iced Tea Packets

4 cups cold water, preferably filtered

4 tablespoons honey

Ice

6 oranges

2 limes

(Optional: extra oranges and limes for garnish)

THE NEXT GREAT RECIPE MIGHT BE YOURS

Share your best at

   / TakeyaUSA

TROPICAL BLACK

spring green

Simple and pure, this Green Chinese Sencha tea brews to a crisp, light and clean flavor. Known as the "first taste of the coming year," its refreshing flavor will bring to mind the tones and feelings of early spring.

Iced tea just got cool™

INGREDIENTS

FOR 2 QUART
ICED TEA MAKER

Makes 8 glasses

**2 TAKEYA Spring
Green Iced Tea Packets**

**4 cups cold water,
preferably filtered**

3 tablespoons honey

Ice

**2/3 cup fresh mint,
chopped**

**2 1/3 cups honeydew,
chopped into
1/2-inch pieces**

(Optional: extra mint
and honeydew for garnish)

honeydew & mint

Use toothpicks to create small fruit and herb
kabobs. Simply layer mint and honeydew cubes
on toothpicks or drink stirrers, and add to each
glass before serving.

1. PREP Tear open the TAKEYA Spring Green Iced Tea Packets,
pour tea into Tea Infuser and twist into lid.

2. BREW Heat water to a boil, cool for 4 minutes and fill the pitcher
halfway. Lower the lid with attached Tea Infuser into the hot water,
allowing steam to vent, and brew for 3 minutes. Remove the lid and
detach the Tea Infuser. Stir in honey until dissolved.

3. FLASH CHILL Top off with ice, seal lid and shake for 30 seconds
to flash chill. Remove 1 1/3 cups of the iced tea to make room for the
fruit infusion.

4. ADD FRUIT & HERB FLAVORS Twist the Fruit Infuser into the
Infuser Extender and add chopped mint and honeydew. Twist the
Fruit Infuser into the lid, lower it into the iced tea and seal airtight.
Zip on the Thermo Jacket and infuse for 3 hours in the refrigerator
before serving.

FAST FRUIT BLEND ALTERNATIVE *Add 1 cup chopped mint to
the bottom of the pitcher and muddle with a wooden spoon. Follow the
steps above to brew, sweeten (using 4 tablespoons honey) and chill
the iced tea. Remove 2 cups of the iced tea. Add 2 cups blended honeydew.
Seal lid and shake to mix before serving.*

coconut & ginger

Love coconut? Swap plain water with 4 cups of coconut water for a seriously hydrating sip. Use water straight from the coconut or purchase an unsweetened bottle, available at most grocery stores. Simply heat the coconut water to a boil, cool for 4 minutes and fill the pitcher halfway before brewing.

1. PREP Tear open the TAKEYA Spring Green Iced Tea Packets, pour tea into Tea Infuser and twist into lid.

2. BREW Heat water to a boil, cool for 4 minutes and fill the pitcher halfway. Lower the lid with attached Tea Infuser into the hot water, allowing steam to vent, and brew for 3 minutes. Remove the lid and detach the Tea Infuser. Stir in honey until dissolved.

3. FLASH CHILL Top off with ice, seal lid and shake for 30 seconds to flash chill. Remove 1⅓ cups of the iced tea to make room for the fruit infusion.

4. ADD FRUIT FLAVOR Twist the Fruit Infuser into the Infuser Extender and add chopped coconut and sliced ginger. Twist the Fruit Infuser into the lid, lower it into the iced tea and seal airtight. Zip on the Thermo Jacket and infuse for 3 hours in the refrigerator before serving.

FAST FRUIT BLEND ALTERNATIVE *Add 5-inch piece sliced ginger to the bottom of the pitcher and muddle with a wooden spoon. Follow the steps above to brew, sweeten and chill the iced tea. Remove 1½ cups of the iced tea. Add 1½ cups unsweetened and chilled coconut water. Seal lid and shake to mix before serving.*

INGREDIENTS

FOR 2 QUART
ICED TEA MAKER
Makes 8 glasses

2 TAKEYA Spring Green Iced Tea Packets

4 cups cold water, preferably filtered

4 tablespoons honey

Ice

2 cups fresh coconut, shell removed & chopped into ½-inch pieces

6-inch piece ginger, thinly sliced

SPRING GREEN

sparkling cherries

Swap fresh cherries for frozen (unsweetened) to eliminate the need to remove pits before infusing. Just remember to let the cherries defrost before chopping and adding them to the infuser.

1. PREP Tear open the TAKEYA Spring Green Iced Tea Packets, pour tea into Tea Infuser and twist into lid.

2. BREW Heat water to a boil, cool for 4 minutes and fill the pitcher halfway. Lower the lid with attached Tea Infuser into the hot water, allowing steam to vent, and brew for 3 minutes. Remove the lid and detach the Tea Infuser. Stir in honey until dissolved.

3. FLASH CHILL Top off with ice, seal lid and shake for 30 seconds to flash chill. Remove 1½ cups of the iced tea to make room for the fruit infusion.

4. ADD FRUIT FLAVOR Twist the Fruit Infuser into the Infuser Extender and add chopped cherries. Twist the Fruit Infuser into the lid, lower it into the iced tea and seal airtight. Zip on the Thermo Jacket and infuse for 3 hours in the refrigerator. Before serving, fill each glass ¾ full with iced tea and top off with a splash of sparkling water for a fizzy effect.

FAST JUICE ALTERNATIVE *Follow the steps above to brew, sweeten and chill the iced tea. Remove 1½ cups of the iced tea. Add 1½ cups unsweetened and chilled cherry juice. Seal lid and shake to mix. Before serving, fill each glass ¾ full with iced tea and top off with a splash of sparkling water for a fizzy effect.*

INGREDIENTS

FOR 2 QUART
ICED TEA MAKER

Makes 8 glasses

2 TAKEYA Spring Green Iced Tea Packets

4 cups cold water, preferably filtered

2 tablespoons honey

Ice

3 cups cherries, pitted and chopped

1 small bottle sparkling water (approx. 16.9 oz.)

SPRING GREEN

INGREDIENTS

FOR 2 QUART
ICED TEA MAKER

Makes 8 glasses

**2 TAKEYA Spring
Green Iced Tea Packets**

**4 cups cold water,
preferably filtered**

4 tablespoons honey

Ice

**1¾ cups strawberries,
stems removed, chopped
into ½-inch pieces**

**1 cup kiwi, peeled
and chopped into
½-inch pieces**

strawberry & kiwi

Not familiar with peeling a kiwi? Slice the fruit
in half and run a spoon around the edge to easily
scoop out the kiwi.

1. PREP Tear open the TAKEYA Spring Green Iced Tea Packets,
pour tea into Tea Infuser and twist into lid.

2. BREW Heat water to a boil, cool for 4 minutes and fill the pitcher
halfway. Lower the lid with attached Tea Infuser into the hot water,
allowing steam to vent, and brew for 3 minutes. Remove the lid and
detach the Tea Infuser. Stir in honey until dissolved.

3. FLASH CHILL Top off with ice, seal lid and shake for 30 seconds
to flash chill. Remove 1⅓ cups of the iced tea to make room for the
fruit infusion.

4. ADD FRUIT FLAVOR Twist the Fruit Infuser into the Infuser Extender
and add chopped strawberries and kiwi to the Fruit Infuser. Twist the
Fruit Infuser into the lid, lower it into the iced tea and seal airtight.
Zip on the Thermo Jacket and infuse for 3 hours in the refrigerator
before serving.

FAST BLEND ALTERNATIVE *Follow the steps above to brew, sweeten
and chill the iced tea. Remove 2 cups of the iced tea. Add 1½ cups
blended strawberries and ½ cup blended kiwi. Seal lid and shake to
mix before serving.*

pear, lemon & ginger

While every pear variety will infuse to reveal a delicate fruit flavor, we recommend Bosc for its crisp, sweet flavor or Bartlett for its extra juicy fruit.

1. PREP Add sliced ginger to bottom of the pitcher and muddle with a wooden spoon. Tear open the TAKEYA Spring Green Iced Tea Packets, pour tea into Tea Infuser and twist into lid.

2. BREW Heat water to a boil, cool for 4 minutes and fill the pitcher halfway. Lower the lid with attached Tea Infuser into the hot water, allowing steam to vent, and brew for 3 minutes. Remove the lid and detach the Tea Infuser. Stir in honey until dissolved.

3. FLASH CHILL Top off with ice, seal lid and shake for 30 seconds to flash chill. Remove 1¾ cups of the iced tea to make room for the fruit infusion.

4. ADD CITRUS FLAVOR Twist the Citrus Juicer into the top of the pitcher and juice the lemons. Twist off the Citrus Juicer, seal and shake to mix.

5. ADD FRUIT FLAVOR Twist the Fruit Infuser into the Infuser Extender and add chopped pear. Twist the Fruit Infuser into the lid, lower it into the iced tea and seal airtight. Zip on the Thermo Jacket and infuse for 3 hours in the refrigerator.

INGREDIENTS

FOR 2 QUART
ICED TEA MAKER

Makes 8 glasses

5-inch piece ginger, thinly sliced

2 TAKEYA Spring Green Iced Tea Packets

4 cups cold water, preferably filtered

4½ tablespoons honey

Ice

2 lemons

2¾ cups pear, chopped into ½-inch pieces

SPRING GREEN

INGREDIENTS

FOR 2 QUART
ICED TEA MAKER

Makes 8 glasses

1 cup fresh mint, chopped

½ cup fresh basil, chopped

2 TAKEYA Spring Green Iced Tea Packets

4 cups cold water, preferably filtered

11 tablespoons honey

Ice

6 lemons

2 cups strawberries, stems removed, chopped into ½-inch pieces

strawberry, basil & mint lemonade

Basil might seem like an unusual ingredient for lemonade, but this earthy herb refreshes the palate while balancing the sweet strawberries, vibrant mint and tart lemon.

1. PREP Add chopped mint and basil to the bottom of the pitcher and muddle with a wooden spoon. Tear open the TAKEYA Spring Green Iced Tea Packets, pour tea into Tea Infuser and twist into lid.

2. BREW Heat water to a boil, cool for 4 minutes and fill the pitcher halfway. Lower the lid with attached Tea Infuser into the hot water, allowing steam to vent, and brew for 3 minutes. Remove the lid and detach the Tea Infuser. Stir in honey until dissolved.

3. FLASH CHILL Top off with ice, seal lid and shake for 30 seconds to flash chill. Remove 2⅓ cups of the iced tea to make room for fruit infusion.

4. ADD CITRUS FLAVOR Twist the Citrus Juicer into the top of the pitcher and juice the lemons (rinse off Citrus Juicer halfway through juicing to remove pulp and seeds). Twist off the Citrus Juicer, seal and shake to mix.

5. ADD FRUIT & HERB FLAVORS Twist the Fruit Infuser into the Infuser Extender and add chopped strawberries. Twist the Fruit Infuser into the lid, lower it into the iced tea and seal airtight. Zip on the Thermo Jacket and infuse for 3 hours in the refrigerator.

clementine & tangerine

Serving this citrus-infused sip at a dinner party? Use the petite citrus fruit as a fun and festive base for place cards. Punch a small hole in the corner of a paper place card and tie it, with twine or ribbon, to the fruit. It also doubles as a healthy parting gift.

1. PREP Tear open the TAKEYA Spring Green Iced Tea Packets, pour tea into Tea Infuser and twist into lid.

2. BREW Heat water to a boil, cool for 4 minutes and fill the pitcher halfway. Lower the lid with attached Tea Infuser into the hot water, allowing steam to vent, and brew for 3 minutes. Remove the lid and detach the Tea Infuser. Stir in honey until dissolved.

3. FLASH CHILL Top off with ice, seal lid and shake for 30 seconds to flash chill. Remove 1 cup of the iced tea to make room for citrus juice.

4. ADD CITRUS FLAVOR Twist the Citrus Juicer into the top of the pitcher and juice the clementines and tangerines (rinse off Citrus Juicer halfway through juicing to remove pulp and seeds). Twist off the Citrus Juicer, seal and shake to mix before serving. Zip on the Thermo Jacket.

INGREDIENTS

FOR 2 QUART
ICED TEA MAKER

Makes 8 glasses

2 TAKEYA Spring Green Iced Tea Packets

4 cups cold water, preferably filtered

2 tablespoons honey

Ice

6 clementines

4 tangerines

THE NEXT GREAT RECIPE MIGHT BE YOURS

Share your best at

  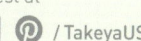 / TakeyaUSA

SPRING GREEN

mintopia green

Watch as these tightly coiled pearls unfurl in the Tea Infuser, revealing fragrant sweet and smoky aromas. Blended with naturally sweet spearmint and peppermint, each full-bodied, bright and refreshing sip will invigorate your senses.

Iced tea just got cool™

INGREDIENTS

FOR 2 QUART
ICED TEA MAKER

Makes 8 glasses

**2 TAKEYA Mintopia
Green Iced Tea Packets**

**4 cups cold water,
preferably filtered**

4 tablespoons honey

Ice

1 lime

**2¾ cups watermelon,
chopped into
½-inch pieces**

**⅔ cup fresh mint,
chopped**

(Optional: extra watermelon
for garnish)

watermelon, lime & mint

To get an even bigger watermelon kick from this drink, fill glasses with frozen watermelon cubes just before serving the Green Mint iced tea infusion. Just slice watermelon into 1-inch cubes and freeze until solid.

1. PREP Tear open the TAKEYA Mintopia Green Iced Tea Packets, pour tea into Tea Infuser and twist into lid.

2. BREW Heat water to a boil, cool for 3 minutes and fill the pitcher halfway. Lower the lid with attached Tea Infuser into the hot water, allowing steam to vent, and brew for 3 minutes. Remove the lid and detach the Tea Infuser. Stir in honey until dissolved.

3. FLASH CHILL Top off with ice, seal lid and shake for 30 seconds to flash chill. Remove 2½ cups of the iced tea to make room for the fruit infusion.

4. ADD CITRUS FLAVOR Twist the Citrus Juicer into the top of the pitcher and juice the lime. Twist off the Citrus Juicer, seal and shake to mix.

5. ADD FRUIT & HERB FLAVORS Twist the Fruit Infuser into the Infuser Extender and add chopped watermelon and mint. Twist the Fruit Infuser into the lid, lower it into the iced tea and seal airtight. Zip on the Thermo Jacket and infuse for 3 hours in the refrigerator.

FOOD PAIRING *Bring on the spices and pair curry, pepper and hot sauces with the sweet and refreshing flavors of watermelon, lime and mint.*

honey & mint limeade

The naturally sweet mint and rich honey balance the zesty lime for a simple sip bursting with flavor. Be sure to pick up a few extra mint sprigs to garnish each glass (add more sprigs to small glass vases for aromatic décor).

1. PREP Add chopped mint to the bottom of the pitcher and muddle with a wooden spoon. Tear open the TAKEYA Mintopia Green Iced Tea Packets, pour tea into Tea Infuser and twist into lid.

2. BREW Heat water to a boil, cool for 3 minutes and fill the pitcher halfway. Lower the lid with attached Tea Infuser into the hot water, allowing steam to vent, and brew for 3 minutes. Remove the lid and detach the Tea Infuser. Stir in honey until dissolved.

3. FLASH CHILL Top off with ice, seal lid and shake for 30 seconds to flash chill. Remove ¾ cup of the iced tea to make room for the citrus juice.

4. ADD CITRUS FLAVOR Twist the Citrus Juicer into the top of the pitcher and juice the limes. Twist off the Citrus Juicer, seal and shake to mix before serving. Zip on the Thermo Jacket.

TAKEYA TIP *Really love limes? Juice a few more for extra tang, but be sure to remove at least 1 cup of the iced tea before adding the fresh squeezed juice.*

INGREDIENTS

FOR 2 QUART
ICED TEA MAKER
Makes 8 glasses

2 cups fresh mint, chopped

2 TAKEYA Mintopia Green Iced Tea Packets

4 cups cold water, preferably filtered

6 tablespoons honey

Ice

3 limes

(Optional: extra mint for garnish)

INGREDIENTS

FOR 2 QUART
ICED TEA MAKER

Makes 8 glasses

**2 TAKEYA Mintopia
Green Iced Tea Packets**

**4 cups cold water,
preferably filtered**

3 tablespoons honey

Ice

**1 cup honeydew, chopped
into ½-inch pieces**

**1⅓ cups cantaloupe,
chopped into
½-inch pieces**

honeydew & cantaloupe

You won't need the whole melon for this refreshing infusion, so try serving it with a fruit salad made with the remaining honeydew and cantaloupe for the perfect pairing. If fruit salad isn't your cup of tea, pick up smaller quantities of pre-cut, packaged melon.

1. PREP Tear open the TAKEYA Mintopia Green Iced Tea Packets, pour tea into Tea Infuser and twist into lid.

2. BREW Heat water to a boil, cool for 3 minutes and fill the pitcher halfway. Lower the lid with attached Tea Infuser into the hot water, allowing steam to vent, and brew for 3 minutes. Remove the lid and detach the Tea Infuser. Stir in honey until dissolved.

3. FLASH CHILL Top off with ice, seal lid and shake for 30 seconds to flash chill. Remove 1½ cups of the iced tea to make room for the fruit infusion.

4. ADD FRUIT FLAVOR Twist the Fruit Infuser into the Infuser Extender and add chopped honeydew and cantaloupe. Twist the Fruit Infuser into the lid, lower it into the iced tea and seal airtight. Zip on the Thermo Jacket and infuse for 3 hours in the refrigerator.

FAST FRUIT BLEND ALTERNATIVE *Follow the steps above to brew, sweeten and chill the iced tea. Remove 2½ cups of the iced tea. Add 1½ cups blended cantaloupe and 1 cup blended honeydew. Seal lid and shake to mix before serving.*

grapefruit & lime

Wake up on the right side of the bed with this bright, citrusy infusion featuring your daily dose of freshly squeezed grapefruit juice.

1. PREP Tear open the TAKEYA Mintopia Green Iced Tea Packets, pour tea into Tea Infuser and twist into lid.

2. BREW Heat water to a boil, cool for 3 minutes and fill the pitcher halfway. Lower the lid with attached Tea Infuser into the hot water, allowing steam to vent, and brew for 3 minutes. Remove the lid and detach the Tea Infuser. Stir in honey until dissolved.

3. FLASH CHILL Top off with ice, seal lid and shake for 30 seconds to flash chill. Remove 2¼ cups of the iced tea to make room for the citrus juice.

4. ADD CITRUS FLAVOR Twist the Citrus Juicer into the top of the pitcher and juice the grapefruits and lime (rinse off Citrus Juicer halfway through juicing to remove pulp and seeds). Twist off the Citrus Juicer, seal and shake to mix before serving. Zip on the Thermo Jacket.

INGREDIENTS

FOR 2 QUART
ICED TEA MAKER
Makes 8 glasses

2 TAKEYA Mintopia Green Iced Tea Packets

4 cups cold water, preferably filtered

8 tablespoons honey

Ice

2 large grapefruits (or 4 small grapefruits)

1 lime

MINTOPIA GREEN

raspberry & strawberry

There's more to drink décor than those miniature paper umbrellas. Serve this berry sip with raspberry ice cubes for a fun burst of color and added chill. Just add one whole raspberry to each ice cube mold, add water and freeze.

1. PREP Tear open the TAKEYA Mintopia Green Iced Tea Packets, pour tea into Tea Infuser and twist into lid.

2. BREW Heat water to a boil, cool for 3 minutes and fill the pitcher halfway. Lower the lid with attached Tea Infuser into the hot water, allowing steam to vent, and brew for 3 minutes. Remove the lid and detach the Tea Infuser. Stir in honey until dissolved.

3. FLASH CHILL Top off with ice, seal lid and shake for 30 seconds to flash chill. Remove 1½ cups of the iced tea to make room for the fruit infusion

4. ADD FRUIT FLAVOR Twist the Fruit Infuser into the Infuser Extender and add chopped strawberries and raspberries. Twist the Fruit Infuser into the lid, lower it into the iced tea and seal airtight. Zip on the Thermo Jacket and infuse for 3 hours in the refrigerator.

FAST BLEND ALTERNATIVE *Follow the steps above to brew, sweeten (use 5 tablespoons of honey) and chill the iced tea. Remove 1¾ cups of sthe iced tea. Add 1 cup blended strawberries and ¾ cup blended raspberries. Seal lid and shake to mix before serving.*

INGREDIENTS

FOR 2 QUART
ICED TEA MAKER
Makes 8 glasses

2 TAKEYA Mintopia Green Iced Tea Packets

4 cups cold water, preferably filtered

4 tablespoons honey

Ice

1½ cups strawberries, stems removed & chopped into ½-inch pieces

1 cup raspberries, chopped

(Optional: extra raspberries for garnish)

MINTOPIA GREEN

INGREDIENTS

FOR 2 QUART
ICED TEA MAKER

Makes 8 glasses

**2 TAKEYA Mintopia
Green Iced Tea Packets**

**4 cups cold water,
preferably filtered**

3 tablespoons honey

Ice

2 oranges

**1½ cups pineapple,
chopped into
½ inch pieces**

**1 cup oranges, peeled
and chopped into
½-inch pieces**

pineapple & orange

Unsure how to pick the perfect pineapple? The easiest way is to use your nose. If it smells sweet and fragrant, then it's ready for infusing.

1. PREP Tear open the TAKEYA Mintopia Green Iced Tea Packets, pour tea into Tea Infuser and twist into lid.

2. BREW Heat water to a boil, cool for 3 minutes and fill the pitcher halfway. Lower the lid with attached Tea Infuser into the hot water, allowing steam to vent, and brew for 3 minutes. Remove the lid and detach the Tea Infuser. Stir in honey until dissolved.

3. FLASH CHILL Top off with ice, seal lid and shake for 30 seconds to flash chill. Remove 1½ cups of the iced tea to make room for fruit infusion.

4. ADD CITRUS FLAVOR Twist the Citrus Juicer into the top of the pitcher and juice 2 oranges. Twist off the Citrus Juicer, seal and shake to mix.

5. ADD FRUIT FLAVOR Twist the Fruit Infuser into the Infuser Extender and add chopped pineapple and orange. Twist the Fruit Infuser into the lid, lower it into the iced tea and seal airtight. Zip on the Thermo Jacket and infuse for 3 hours in the refrigerator.

FAST JUICE ALTERNATIVE *Follow the steps above to brew, sweeten (only use 2 tablespoons honey) and chill the iced tea. Remove 2¼ cups of the iced tea. Add 1 cup unsweetened and chilled pineapple juice and 1¼ cups chilled orange juice. Seal lid and shake to mix before serving.*

lemongrass & ginger

The long, thin, green lemongrass stalk reveals a subtle citrus flavor when the outer leaves are removed and it's finely chopped. Often found in Asian markets, it can also be easily grown at home.

1. PREP Tear open the TAKEYA Mintopia Green Iced Tea Packets, pour tea into Tea Infuser and twist into lid.

2. BREW Heat water to a boil, cool for 3 minutes and fill the pitcher halfway. Lower the lid with attached Tea Infuser into the hot water, allowing steam to vent, and brew for 3 minutes. Remove the lid and detach the Tea Infuser. Stir in honey until dissolved.

3. FLASH CHILL Top off with ice, seal lid and shake for 30 seconds to flash chill. Remove 1⅓ cups of the iced tea to make room for the infusion.

4. ADD FLAVOR Twist the Fruit Infuser into the Infuser Extender and add sliced ginger and chopped lemongrass. Twist the Fruit Infuser into the lid, lower it into the iced tea and seal airtight. Zip on the Thermo Jacket and infuse for 3 hours in the refrigerator.

INGREDIENTS

FOR 2 QUART
ICED TEA MAKER
Makes 8 glasses

2 TAKEYA Mintopia Green Iced Tea Packets

4 cups cold water, preferably filtered

3 tablespoons honey

Ice

8-inch piece of ginger, thinly sliced

1 cup lemongrass (approximately 4 lemongrass stalks), ends trimmed and outer leaves removed, chopped into ½-inch pieces

MINTOPIA GREEN

coconut vibe

Harvested from a plant in South Africa, these caffeine-free Green Rooibos leaves brew to reveal a smooth and clean flavor with a hint of natural sweetness. Earthy green rooibos blends with rich coconut, papaya, pineapple and zesty lime peel to transport you to the tropics.

Iced tea just got cool™

INGREDIENTS

FOR 2 QUART
ICED TEA MAKER

Makes 8 glasses

**2 TAKEYA Coconut
Vibe Iced Tea Packets**

**3 tablespoons dried
coconut flakes/chips
(unsweetened)**

**4 cups cold water,
preferably filtered**

2 tablespoons honey

Ice

2 limes

**2¾ cups pineapple,
chopped into
½-inch pieces**

(Optional: extra pineapple
for garnish)

coconut, pineapple & lime

Add a chilly burst of flavor by filling each glass with
a few frozen pineapple cubes before serving. Simply
chop extra pineapple into 1-inch cubes and freeze
until solid.

1. PREP Tear open the TAKEYA Coconut Vibe Iced Tea Packets, pour into
Tea Infuser along with the dried coconut flakes. Twist the Tea Infuser
into the lid.

2. BREW Heat water to a boil, cool for 1 minute and fill the pitcher halfway.
Lower the lid with attached Tea Infuser into the hot water, allowing steam
to vent, and brew for 7 minutes. Remove the lid and detach the Tea Infuser.
Stir in honey until dissolved.

3. FLASH CHILL Top off with ice, seal lid and shake for 30 seconds to
flash chill. Remove 1½ cups of the iced herbal blend to make room for the
fruit infusion.

4. ADD CITRUS FLAVOR Twist the Citrus Juicer into the top of the pitcher
and juice the limes. Twist off the Citrus Juicer, seal and shake to mix.

5. ADD FRUIT FLAVOR Twist the Fruit Infuser into the Infuser Extender
and add chopped pineapple. Twist the Fruit Infuser into the lid, lower it
into the iced herbal blend and seal airtight. Zip on the Thermo Jacket and
infuse for 3 hours in the refrigerator.

honey clementine

Clementines are the darling of the citrus family and with good reason—they are incredibly flavorful and sweet. Look for them in grocery stores between October and February.

1. PREP Tear open the TAKEYA Coconut Vibe Iced Tea Packets, pour into Tea Infuser and twist into lid.

2. BREW Heat water to a boil, cool for 1 minute and fill the pitcher halfway. Lower the lid with attached Tea Infuser into the hot water, allowing steam to vent, and brew for 7 minutes. Remove the lid and detach the Tea Infuser. Stir in honey until dissolved.

3. FLASH CHILL Top off with ice, seal lid and shake for 30 seconds to flash chill. Remove 1 cup of the iced herbal blend to make room for the citrus juice.

4. ADD CITRUS FLAVOR Twist the Citrus Juicer into the top of the pitcher and juice the clementines. Twist off the Citrus Juicer, seal and shake to mix before serving. Zip on the Thermo Jacket.

INGREDIENTS

FOR 2 QUART
ICED TEA MAKER

Makes 8 glasses

2 TAKEYA Coconut Vibe Iced Tea Packets

4 cups cold water, preferably filtered

4 tablespoons honey

Ice

8 clementines

COCONUT VIBE

INGREDIENTS

FOR 2 QUART
ICED TEA MAKER

Makes 8 glasses

**2 TAKEYA Coconut
Vibe Iced Tea Packets**

**4 cups cold water,
preferably filtered**

3 tablespoons honey

Ice

**1¾ cups mango, chopped
into ½-inch pieces**

**1 cup papaya, chopped
into ½-inch pieces**

Fresh mint, for garnish

papaya, mango & mint

Not quite sure how to pick the perfect papaya? Look for one with yellow skin that offers a light, sweet aroma. It's best to chop the fruit when ripe, and then store it in an airtight container in the refrigerator before infusing.

1. PREP Tear open the TAKEYA Coconut Vibe Iced Tea Packets, pour into Tea Infuser and twist into lid.

2. BREW Heat water to a boil, cool for 1 minute and fill the pitcher halfway. Lower the lid with attached Tea Infuser into the hot water, allowing steam to vent, and brew for 7 minutes. Remove the lid and detach the Tea Infuser. Stir in honey until dissolved.

3. FLASH CHILL Top off with ice, seal lid and shake for 30 seconds to flash chill. Remove 1½ cups of the iced herbal blend to make room for the fruit infusion.

4. ADD FRUIT FLAVOR Twist the Fruit Infuser into the Infuser Extender and add chopped mango and papaya. Twist the Fruit Infuser into the lid, lower it into the iced herbal blend and seal airtight. Zip on the Thermo Jacket and infuse for 3 hours in the refrigerator. Garnish each glass with fresh mint sprigs before serving.

FOOD PAIRING *Smooth, cool cucumber and yogurt soup or chilled coconut gazpacho pair well with this light, tropical iced tea infusion.*

lychee & lime

Highlight the fragrant and floral lychee fruit by creating a simple garnish. Pierce a whole lychee with a drink stirrer or straw, and add to each glass of the iced herbal blend before serving.

1. PREP Tear open the TAKEYA Coconut Vibe Iced Tea Packets, pour into Tea Infuser and twist into lid.

2. BREW Heat water to a boil, cool for 1 minute and fill the pitcher halfway. Lower the lid with attached Tea Infuser into the hot water, allowing steam to vent, and brew for 7 minutes. Remove the lid and detach the Tea Infuser. Stir in honey until dissolved.

3. FLASH CHILL Top off with ice, seal lid and shake for 30 seconds to flash chill. Remove 2½ cups of the iced herbal blend to make room for the fruit infusion.

4. ADD CITRUS FLAVOR Twist the Citrus Juicer into the top of the pitcher and juice the limes. Twist off the Citrus Juicer, seal and shake to mix.

5. ADD FRUIT FLAVOR Add reserved lychee liquid to the pitcher. Twist the Fruit Infuser into Infuser Extender and add chopped lychee fruit. Twist the Fruit Infuser into the lid, lower it into the iced herbal blend and seal airtight. Zip on the Thermo Jacket and infuse for 3 hours in the refrigerator.

FOOD PAIRING *Pair this exotic tea infusion with frozen desserts like lychee sorbet or mango and lime granita.*

INGREDIENTS

FOR 2 QUART
ICED TEA MAKER

Makes 8 glasses

2 TAKEYA Coconut Vibe Iced Tea Packets

4 cups cold water, preferably filtered

3 tablespoons honey

Ice

2 limes

2 20 oz. cans lychee fruit, drained (reserve ½ cup of liquid) and chopped into ½-inch pieces

(Optional: extra can of lychee fruit for garnish)

COCONUT VIBE

blueberry & blackberry

If you fall for this berry sip, then stock up on frozen bags of the sweet and tart fruit. Just be sure to defrost and chop the berries before infusing.

1. PREP Tear open the TAKEYA Coconut Vibe Iced Tea Packets, pour into Tea Infuser and twist into lid.

2. BREW Heat water to a boil, cool for 1 minute and fill the pitcher halfway. Lower the lid with attached Tea Infuser into the hot water, allowing steam to vent, and brew for 7 minutes. Remove the lid and detach the Tea Infuser. Stir in honey until dissolved.

3. FLASH CHILL Top off with ice, seal lid and shake for 30 seconds to flash chill. Remove 1½ cups of the iced herbal blend to make room for the fruit infusion.

4. ADD FRUIT FLAVOR Twist the Fruit Infuser into the Infuser Extender and add chopped berries. Twist the Fruit Infuser into the lid, lower it into the iced herbal blend and seal airtight. Zip on the Thermo Jacket and infuse for 3 hours in the refrigerator.

FAST FRUIT BLEND ALTERNATIVE *Follow the steps above to brew, sweeten and chill the iced herbal blend. Remove 1½ cups of the iced herbal blend. Add 1 cup blended blueberries and ½ cup blended blackberries. Seal lid and shake to mix before serving.*

INGREDIENTS

FOR 2 QUART
ICED TEA MAKER
Makes 8 glasses

2 TAKEYA Coconut Vibe Iced Tea Packets

4 cups cold water, preferably filtered

3 tablespoons honey

Ice

1½ cups blueberries, chopped

1 cup blackberries, chopped

COCONUT VIBE

INGREDIENTS

FOR 2 QUART
ICED TEA MAKER

Makes 8 glasses

**2 TAKEYA Coconut
Vibe Iced Tea Packets**

**4 cups cold water,
preferably filtered**

2 tablespoons honey

Ice

8 oranges

**3 cups fresh coconut,
shell removed, chopped
into ½-inch pieces**

coconut orangeade

Prepping for a party? Crack the hard coconut shell
ahead of time. Store sliced coconut in a plastic bag
in the fridge for up to two days before infusing.

1. PREP Tear open the TAKEYA Coconut Vibe Iced Tea Packets,
pour into Tea Infuser and twist into lid.

2. BREW Heat water to a boil, cool for 1 minute and fill the pitcher
halfway. Lower the lid with attached Tea Infuser into the hot water,
allowing steam to vent, and brew for 7 minutes. Remove the lid and
detach the Tea Infuser. Stir in honey until dissolved.

3. FLASH CHILL Top off with ice, seal lid and shake for 30 seconds
to flash chill. Remove 5⅓ cups of the iced herbal blend to make room
for the fruit infusion.

4. ADD CITRUS FLAVOR Twist the Citrus Juicer into the top of the
pitcher and juice the oranges (rinse off Citrus Juicer halfway through
juicing to remove pulp and seeds). Twist off the Citrus Juicer, seal
and shake to mix.

5. ADD FRUIT FLAVOR Twist the Fruit Infuser into the Infuser Extender
and add chopped coconut. Twist the Fruit Infuser into the lid, lower it
into the iced herbal blend and seal airtight. Zip on the Thermo Jacket
and infuse for 3 hours in the refrigerator.

cherry & lime

While fresh cherries are best, pitting them can be tedious. If you're not up to the task, substitute frozen, unsweetened cherries. Be sure to let them defrost before chopping.

1. PREP Tear open the TAKEYA Coconut Vibe Iced Tea Packets, pour into Tea Infuser and twist into lid.

2. BREW Heat water to a boil, cool for 1 minute and fill the pitcher halfway. Lower the lid with attached Tea Infuser into the hot water, allowing steam to vent, and brew for 7 minutes. Remove the lid and detach the Tea Infuser. Stir in honey until dissolved.

3. FLASH CHILL Top off with ice, seal lid and shake for 30 seconds to flash chill. Remove 1¾ cups of the iced herbal blend to make room for the fruit infusion.

4. ADD CITRUS FLAVOR Twist the Citrus Juicer into the top of the pitcher and juice the limes. Twist off the Citrus Juicer, seal and shake to mix.

5. ADD FRUIT FLAVOR Twist the Fruit Infuser into the Infuser Extender and add chopped cherries. Twist the Fruit Infuser into the lid, lower it into the iced herbal blend and seal airtight. Zip on the Thermo Jacket and infuse for 3 hours in the refrigerator.

FAST JUICE ALTERNATIVE *Follow the steps above to brew, sweeten and chill the iced herbal blend. Remove 2¼ cups of the iced herbal blend. Juice 1 lime with the Citrus Juicer. Add 2 cups unsweetened and chilled cherry juice. Seal lid and shake to mix before serving.*

INGREDIENTS

FOR 2 QUART
ICED TEA MAKER
Makes 8 glasses

2 TAKEYA Coconut Vibe Iced Tea Packets

4 cups cold water, preferably filtered

5 tablespoons honey

Ice

2 limes

3 cups cherries, pitted and chopped

THE NEXT GREAT RECIPE MIGHT BE YOURS

Share your best at

  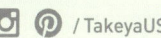 / TakeyaUSA

COCONUT VIBE

hibiscus pomegranate

The rich, tart citrus taste of hibiscus and pomegranate is balanced by fruity and sweet flavors of apple and cherry. This caffeine-free Fruit Blend is perfect for kids as an alternative to artificially sweetened fruit drinks. Watch how the herbal blend quickly transforms the hot water into a vibrant red, naturally hued treat. As beautiful as it is delicious.

Iced tea just got cool™

INGREDIENTS

FOR 2 QUART
ICED TEA MAKER

Makes 8 glasses

**2 TAKEYA Hibiscus
Pomegranate Iced
Tea Packets**

**4 cups cold water,
preferably filtered**

2½ tablespoons honey

Ice

4 blood oranges

**2½ cups cherries, pitted
and chopped**

**1 bottle sparkling water
(approx. 16.9 oz.)**

sparkling cherry
& blood orange

Trying to kick the soda habit? This sparkling iced herbal infusion with bold cherry and blood orange flavors may do the trick.

1. PREP Tear open the TAKEYA Hibiscus Pomegranate Iced Tea Packets, pour into Tea Infuser and twist into lid.

2. BREW Heat water to a boil, cool for 1 minute and fill the pitcher halfway. Lower the lid with attached Tea Infuser into the hot water, allowing steam to vent, and brew for 7 minutes. Remove the lid and detach the Tea Infuser. Stir in honey until dissolved.

3. FLASH CHILL Top off with ice, seal lid and shake for 30 seconds to flash chill. Remove 2 cups of the iced herbal blend to make room for the fruit infusion.

4. ADD CITRUS FLAVOR Twist the Citrus Juicer into the top of the pitcher and juice the blood oranges. Twist off the Citrus Juicer, seal and shake to mix.

5. ADD FRUIT FLAVOR Twist the Fruit Infuser into the Infuser Extender and add chopped cherries. Twist the Fruit Infuser into the lid, lower it into the iced herbal blend and seal airtight. Zip on the Thermo Jacket and infuse for 3 hours in the refrigerator. Before serving, fill each glass ¾ full and top off with a splash of sparkling water.

FAST JUICE ALTERNATIVE *Follow the steps above to brew and chill the iced herbal blend (no honey needed). Remove 2½ cups of the iced herbal blend. Add 1 cup unsweetened and chilled cherry juice. Seal lid and shake to mix. Remove lid and add 1½ cups blood orange Italian soda. Stir before serving but do not shake.*

TAKEYA TIP *Don't feel like pitting cherries? In place of the fresh fruit, use the same amount of frozen pitted cherries.*

strawberry, raspberry & blueberry

Using a toothpick or drink stirrer, layer a blueberry between a strawberry slice and a whole raspberry for a sweet trio garnish. It doubles as a small snack for parties. Make these in the morning and refrigerate until party time. Just be sure to pick up extra berries.

1. PREP Tear open the TAKEYA Hibiscus Pomegranate Iced Tea Packets, pour into Tea Infuser and twist into lid.

2. BREW Heat water to a boil, cool for 1 minute and fill the pitcher halfway. Lower the lid with attached Tea Infuser into the hot water, allowing steam to vent, and brew for 7 minutes. Remove the lid and detach the Tea Infuser. Stir in honey until dissolved.

3. FLASH CHILL Top off with ice, seal lid and shake for 30 seconds to flash chill. Remove 1½ cups of the iced herbal blend to make room for the fruit infusion.

4. ADD FRUIT FLAVOR Twist the Fruit Infuser into the Infuser Extender and add chopped strawberries, blueberries and raspberries. Twist the Fruit Infuser into the lid, lower it into the iced herbal blend and seal airtight. Zip on the Thermo Jacket and infuse for 3 hours in the refrigerator.

INGREDIENTS

FOR 2 QUART
ICED TEA MAKER
Makes 8 glasses

2 TAKEYA Hibiscus Pomegranate Iced Tea Packets

4 cups cold water, preferably filtered

3 tablespoons honey

Ice

1 cup strawberries, stems removed and chopped into ½-inch pieces

1 cup blueberries, chopped

½ cup raspberries, chopped

(Optional: extra berries for garnish)

HIBISCUS POMEGRANATE

INGREDIENTS

FOR 2 QUART
ICED TEA MAKER

Makes 8 glasses

**2 TAKEYA Hibiscus
Pomegranate Iced
Tea Packets**

**4 cups cold water,
preferably filtered**

6 tablespoons honey

Ice

**2 large grapefruits
(or 4 small grapefruits)**

5 oranges

grapefruit orangeade

Surrounded by citrus and not sure which orange
to choose? We recommend the Cara Cara orange
for its rosy hue, low acidity and extra sweet taste.

1. PREP Tear open the TAKEYA Hibiscus Pomegranate Iced Tea Packets,
pour into Tea Infuser and twist into lid.

2. BREW Heat water to a boil, cool for 1 minute and fill the pitcher
halfway. Lower the lid with attached Tea Infuser into the hot water,
allowing steam to vent, and brew for 7 minutes. Remove the lid and
detach the Tea Infuser. Stir in honey until dissolved.

3. FLASH CHILL Top off with ice, seal lid and shake for 30 seconds
to flash chill. Remove 3½ cups of the iced herbal blend to make room
for the citrus juice.

4. ADD CITRUS FLAVOR Twist the Citrus Juicer into the top of the
pitcher and juice the grapefruits and oranges (rinse off Citrus Juicer
occasionally during juicing to remove pulp and seeds). Twist off
the Citrus Juicer, seal and shake to mix before serving. Zip on the
TAKEYA Thermo Jacket.

cran-raspberry

Only found in the produce section from October through December, cranberries are often available in the frozen fruit aisle.

1. PREP Tear open the TAKEYA Hibiscus Pomegranate Iced Tea Packets, pour into Tea Infuser and twist into lid.

2. BREW Heat water to a boil, cool for 1 minute and fill the pitcher halfway. Lower the lid with attached Tea Infuser into the hot water, allowing steam to vent, and brew for 7 minutes. Remove the lid and detach the Tea Infuser. Stir in honey until dissolved.

3. FLASH CHILL Top off with ice, seal lid and shake for 30 seconds to flash chill. Remove 1⅓ cups of the iced herbal blend to make room for fruit infusion.

4. ADD FRUIT FLAVOR Twist the Fruit Infuser into Infuser Extender and add chopped cranberries and raspberries. Twist the Fruit Infuser into the lid, lower it into the iced herbal blend and seal airtight. Zip on the Thermo Jacket and infuse for 3 hours in the refrigerator.

FAST JUICE ALTERNATIVE *Follow the steps above to brew and chill the iced herbal blend (no honey needed). Remove 2 cups of the iced herbal blend. Add 2 cups chilled cran-raspberry juice blend. Seal lid and shake to mix before serving.*

INGREDIENTS

FOR 2 QUART
ICED TEA MAKER

Makes 8 glasses

2 TAKEYA Hibiscus Pomegranate Iced Tea Packets

4 cups cold water, preferably filtered

4 tablespoons honey

Ice

1½ cups cranberries, chopped

1 cup raspberries, chopped

HIBISCUS POMEGRANATE

grapefruit & pomegranate

To easily remove seeds from a pomegranate, cut it into quarters and immerse in a bowl of cold water. While breaking apart the fruit under water, the seeds will sink to the bottom and the membrane will float to the top for easy removal. You can also purchase containers of fresh pomegranate seeds at most grocery stores in the produce section.

1. PREP Tear open the TAKEYA Hibiscus Pomegranate Iced Tea Packets, pour into Tea Infuser and twist into lid.

2. BREW Heat water to a boil, cool for 1 minute and fill the pitcher halfway. Lower the lid with attached Tea Infuser into the hot water, allowing steam to vent, and brew for 7 minutes. Remove the lid and detach the Tea Infuser. Stir in honey until dissolved.

3. FLASH CHILL Top off with ice, seal lid and shake for 30 seconds to flash chill. Remove 2¼ cups of the iced herbal blend to make room for the fruit infusion.

4. ADD CITRUS FLAVOR Twist the Citrus Juicer into the top of the pitcher and juice the grapefruits. Twist off the Citrus Juicer, seal and shake to mix.

5. ADD FRUIT FLAVOR Twist the Fruit Infuser into the Infuser Extender and add the pomegranate seeds. Twist the Fruit Infuser into the lid, lower it into the iced herbal blend and seal airtight. Zip on the Thermo Jacket and infuse for 3 hours in the refrigerator.

FAST JUICE ALTERNATIVE *Follow the steps above to brew, sweeten and chill the iced herbal blend. Remove 2 cups of the iced herbal blend. Add 1 cup chilled grapefruit juice and 1 cup unsweetened and chilled pomegranate juice. Seal lid and shake to mix before serving.*

FOOD PAIRING *Pick up an extra pomegranate and sprinkle the seeds onto a green salad with grapefruit slices and a honey vinaigrette.*

INGREDIENTS

FOR 2 QUART
ICED TEA MAKER
Makes 8 glasses

2 TAKEYA Hibiscus Pomegranate Iced Tea Packets

4 cups water, preferably filtered

5 tablespoons honey

Ice

2 large grapefruits (or 4 small grapefruits)

18 tablespoons pomegranate seeds

HIBISCUS POMEGRANATE

INGREDIENTS

FOR 2 QUART
ICED TEA MAKER
Makes 8 glasses

4 cups fresh mint, chopped

2 TAKEYA Hibiscus Pomegranate Iced Tea Packets

4 cups cold water, preferably filtered

9 tablespoons honey

Ice

5 lemons

hibiscus & mint lemonade

Help your kids make the switch from artificial, sugary drinks to a healthier sip with this fruity and tangy lemonade sweetened with all-natural honey. Even before they fall for the flavors, the bright red hue will draw them in.

1. PREP Add chopped mint to the bottom of the pitcher and muddle with a wooden spoon. Tear open the TAKEYA Hibiscus Pomegranate Iced Tea Packets, pour into Tea Infuser and twist into lid.

2. BREW Heat water to a boil, cool for 1 minute and fill the pitcher halfway. Lower the lid with attached Tea Infuser into the hot water, allowing steam to vent, and brew for 7 minutes. Remove the lid and detach the Tea Infuser. Stir in honey until dissolved.

3. FLASH CHILL Top off with ice, seal lid and shake for 30 seconds to flash chill. Remove 1⅓ cups of the iced herbal blend to make room for citrus infusion.

4. ADD CITRUS FLAVOR Twist the Citrus Juicer into the top of the pitcher and juice the lemons. Twist off the Citrus Juicer, seal and shake to mix before serving. Zip on the TAKEYA Thermo Jacket.

FOOD PAIRING *Bring out the kid in everyone and serve this fruity lemonade with classic hamburgers, hot dogs and French fries.*

HIBISCUS POMEGRANATE

apple orangeade

Your favorite apple will do, but we recommend infusing the Honeycrisp variety for its incredibly crisp and sweet flavor.

1. PREP Tear open the TAKEYA Hibiscus Pomegranate Iced Tea Packets, pour into Tea Infuser and twist into lid.

2. BREW Heat water to a boil, cool for 1 minute and fill the pitcher halfway. Lower the lid with attached Tea Infuser into the hot water, allowing steam to vent, and brew for 7 minutes. Remove the lid and detach the Tea Infuser. Stir in honey until dissolved.

3. FLASH CHILL Top off with ice, seal lid and shake for 30 seconds to flash chill. Remove 3⅓ cups of the iced herbal blend to make room for fruit infusion.

4. ADD CITRUS FLAVOR Twist the Citrus Juicer into the top of the pitcher and juice the oranges. Twist off the Citrus Juicer, seal and shake to mix.

5. ADD FRUIT FLAVOR Twist the Fruit Infuser into the Infuser Extender and add chopped apple. Twist the Fruit Infuser into the lid, lower it into the iced herbal blend and seal airtight. Zip on the Thermo Jacket and infuse for 3 hours in the refrigerator.

INGREDIENTS

FOR 2 QUART
ICED TEA MAKER
Makes 8 glasses

2 TAKEYA Hibiscus Pomegranate Iced Tea Packets

4 cups cold water, preferably filtered

3 tablespoons honey

Ice

4 oranges

3 cups red apple, chopped into ½-inch pieces

THE NEXT GREAT RECIPE MIGHT BE YOURS
Share your best at
   / TakeyaUSA

HIBISCUS POMEGRANATE

fruit infusions & citrus juice blends

In addition to making loose leaf iced tea, you can also create easy fruit-based infusions. Using the Fruit Infuser and Citrus Juicer accessories, whip up refreshing, all natural fruit-infused water and citrus juice blends every day.

FROM LEFT TO RIGHT

INGREDIENTS

FOR 2 QUART
ICED TEA MAKER

Makes 8 glasses

6 cups hot water

2 tablespoons honey

1 cup mango, chopped into ½-inch pieces

1½ cups pineapple, chopped into ½-inch pieces

pineapple & mango

You won't need the whole pineapple for this refreshing infusion, so try serving it with a fruit salad made with the remaining pineapple and extra mango. If fruit salad isn't your cup of tea, pick up smaller quantities of pre-cut, packaged fruit in the produce section of your grocery store.

1. PREP Fill ¾ of the pitcher with hot water. Stir in honey until dissolved.

2. ADD FRUIT FLAVOR Twist the Fruit Infuser into the Infuser Extender and add chopped mango and pineapple. Twist the Fruit Infuser into the lid, seal airtight, zip on the Thermo Jacket and infuse for 3 hours in the refrigerator before serving.

grapefruit & orange

Mornings just seem brighter with this citrus duo that's packed with both sweet and tart flavors.

1. PREP Add two cups of hot water to the pitcher. Stir in honey until dissolved.

2. ADD CITRUS FLAVOR Twist the Citrus Juicer into the top of the pitcher and juice the grapefruits and oranges (rinse off Citrus Juicer halfway through juicing to remove pulp and seeds).

3. FLASH CHILL Twist off the Citrus Juicer and top off with ice, seal lid and shake for 30 seconds to flash chill before serving. Zip on the Thermo Jacket.

INGREDIENTS

FOR 2 QUART
ICED TEA MAKER

Makes 8 glasses

2 cups hot water

8 tablespoons honey

4 large grapefruits

4 oranges

Ice

FRUIT INFUSIONS AND CITRUS JUICE BLENDS

green apple, pear & ginger

A whole new take on apple juice, this infusion provides a lightly spiced, incredibly delicious beverage for all ages.

1. PREP Fill ¾ of the pitcher with hot water. Stir in honey until dissolved.

2. ADD FRUIT FLAVOR Twist the Fruit Infuser into the Infuser Extender and add chopped pear, green apple and thinly sliced ginger. Twist the Fruit Infuser into the lid, seal airtight, zip on the Thermo Jacket and infuse for 3 hours in the refrigerator before serving.

INGREDIENTS

FOR 2 QUART
ICED TEA MAKER

Makes 8 glasses

6 cups hot water

3 tablespoons honey

1 cup pear, chopped into ½-inch pieces

1 cup green apple, chopped into ½-inch pieces

4-inch piece ginger, thinly sliced

FRUIT INFUSIONS AND CITRUS JUICE BLENDS

INGREDIENTS

FOR 2 QUART
ICED TEA MAKER

Makes 8 glasses

2 cups hot water

8 tablespoons honey

9 blood oranges

2 limes

Ice

blood orange limeade

Stay refreshed with this bright and bold citrus infusion. The deep red color makes it the perfect party punch. Keep in mind that blood oranges are available from December through April.

1. PREP Add two cups of hot water to the pitcher. Stir in honey until dissolved.

2. ADD CITRUS FLAVOR Twist the Citrus Juicer into the top of the pitcher and juice the blood oranges and limes (rinse off Citrus Juicer during juicing to remove pulp and seeds).

3. FLASH CHILL Twist off the Citrus Juicer and top off with ice, seal lid and shake for 30 seconds to flash chill before serving. Zip on the Thermo Jacket.

INGREDIENTS

FOR 2 QUART
ICED TEA MAKER

Makes 8 glasses

6 cups hot water

2 limes

⅔ cup fresh mint, chopped

2¾ cups watermelon, chopped into ½-inch pieces

watermelon limeade

Cool off with this lightly sweet and fresh citrus infusion. Keep it easy by picking up a seedless watermelon.

1. PREP Fill ¾ of the pitcher with hot water.

2. ADD CITRUS FLAVOR Twist the Citrus Juicer into the top of the pitcher and juice the limes. Twist off the Citrus Juicer, seal and shake to mix.

3. ADD FRUIT FLAVOR Twist the Fruit Infuser into the Infuser Extender and add chopped mint and watermelon. Twist the Fruit Infuser into the lid, seal airtight, zip on the Thermo Jacket and infuse for 3 hours in the refrigerator before serving.

strawberry herb lemonade

Refreshing mint, earthy basil and sweet strawberries pair with honey and fresh lemon juice for the ultimate thirst quencher. To get a pretty pink hue, let the strawberries infuse overnight.

1. PREP Add chopped mint and basil to the bottom of the pitcher and muddle with a wooden spoon. Add four cups of hot water to the pitcher. Stir in honey until dissolved.

2. ADD CITRUS FLAVOR Twist the Citrus Juicer into the top of the pitcher and juice the lemons (rinse off Citrus Juicer during juicing to remove pulp and seeds).

3. FLASH CHILL Twist off the Citrus Juicer and Top off with ice, seal lid and shake for 30 seconds. Remove 1½ cups of the lemonade to make room for the fruit infusion.

3. ADD FRUIT FLAVOR Twist the Fruit Infuser into the Infuser Extender and add chopped strawberries. Twist the Fruit Infuser into the lid, seal airtight, zip on the Thermo Jacket and infuse for 3 hours in the refrigerator before serving.

INGREDIENTS

FOR 2 QUART
ICED TEA MAKER
Makes 8 glasses

1 cup fresh mint, chopped

½ cup fresh basil, chopped

4 cups hot water

11 tablespoons honey

6 lemons

Ice

2 cups strawberries, stems removed, chopped into ½-inch pieces

FRUIT INFUSIONS AND CITRUS JUICE BLENDS

INGREDIENTS

FOR 2 QUART
ICED TEA MAKER

Makes 8 glasses

4 cups hot water

10 tablespoons honey

6 lemons

Ice

classic lemonade

Get back to basics. Skip the frozen concentrate and enjoy the simple pleasure of fresh-squeezed, home-made lemonade sweetened with all-natural honey.

1. PREP Add 4 cups of hot water to the pitcher. Stir in honey until dissolved.

2. ADD CITRUS FLAVOR Twist the Citrus Juicer into the top of the pitcher and juice the lemons (rinse off Citrus Juicer halfway through juicing to remove pulp and seeds).

3. FLASH CHILL Twist off the Citrus Juicer and top off with ice, seal lid and shake for 30 seconds to flash chill before serving. Zip on the Thermo Jacket.

peach, plum & cinnamon

Enjoy this spicy stone fruit drink when the fruits are at their sweetest peak, between May and October.

1. PREP Fill ¾ of the pitcher with hot water. Stir in honey until dissolved.

2. ADD FRUIT & SPICE FLAVORS Twist the Fruit Infuser into the Infuser Extender and add cinnamon sticks, chopped peaches and plums. Twist the Fruit Infuser into the lid, seal airtight, zip on the Thermo Jacket and infuse for 3 hours in the refrigerator before serving.

INGREDIENTS

FOR 2 QUART
ICED TEA MAKER

Makes 8 glasses

6 cups hot water

2 tablespoons honey

5 cinnamon sticks

1½ cups peaches, chopped into ½-inch pieces

1 cup plums, chopped into ½-inch pieces

THE NEXT GREAT RECIPE MIGHT BE YOURS

Share your best at

   / TakeyaUSA

FRUIT INFUSIONS AND CITRUS JUICE BLENDS

index

the next great recipe might be yours

Share your best at / TakeyaUSA